# *saving* MAINE

AN ALBUM OF
*Conservation*
*Success Stories*

# *saving* MAINE

AN ALBUM OF
*Conservation*
*Success Stories*

BILL SILLIKER JR.

*Down East Books*

CAMDEN, MAINE

Book design by Harrah Lord, Yellow House Studio

Printed in China

OGP

5    4    3    2    1


Down East Books / Camden Maine

www.downeastbooks.com

Book orders: (800) 766-1670

*Title page image:*  Logging road near Kokadjo

# *Dedication*

*In memory of Percival P. Baxter, who had*

*the wisdom, foresight, and generosity to make a*

*difference in saving the best of the Maine woods.*

*Every time I witness the wonders of the*

*park that he gave to the people of Maine,*

*I say a quiet "thank you."*

# Contents

9    INTRODUCTION: IS MAINE VANISHING?

16    NATURE AT PEACE
*Percival Baxter and the Creation of Baxter State Park*

24    THE GOLD COAST
*The Founders of Acadia National Park*

33    OLD GROWTH
*The Nature Conservancy Protects Big Reed Forest Reserve*

40    THE BOLD COAST
*The Maine Coast Heritage Trust Comes of Age*

48    A FRIEND IN NEED
*Protecting Goosefare Marsh, in the Rachel Carson National Wildlife Refuge*

56    POLITICAL WILL AND PUBLIC GOOD
*The Land for Maine's Future Program*

64    WHOSE WOODS ARE THESE?
*Enlightened Forest Management*

72    THE LOGGER, THE DAM BREAKER, AND THE WIDGET MAKER
*Individuals Who Make a Difference*

80    A LEGACY THAT LASTS
*The Nature Conservancy Protects the St. John River*

88    CONCLUSION

91    APPENDIX AND ACKNOWLEDGMENTS

—Canoeist at Kidney Pond, Baxter State Park—

# Introduction

**IN AMERICA'S NORTHEAST CORNER, THERE IS A SPECIAL PLACE.**

Much of it is a wild place, blessed with a unique diversity of rugged geography and natural splendor. Thousands of miles of rocky coastline interspersed with a few dozen miles of sandy beaches define its border with the sea. A nearly impenetrable boreal forest, broken by pristine lakes, boggy wetlands, and glacier-scalped mountains, comprises much of its interior.

A handful of nutrient-rich saltwater estuaries strung along its coast support myriad fish, birds, and mammals. Four major rivers, dozens of smaller ones, and hundreds of brooks and streams supply similar sustenance for other wildlife species. Countless islands dot its coast and provide nesting sanctuaries for a magnificent variety of seabirds and waterfowl.

Because of the extraordinary range of habitats in this place, species as diverse as the osprey and the harbor seal, the moose and the black bear all thrive here.

Where is this place? By what name is it called? Maine.

Centuries of human action have had an impact on this place. We have cut most of its tallest trees. We have dammed most of its largest rivers. We have filled some of its wetlands. Yet much of what makes Maine so special still exists. Many miles of its coast remain almost as wild today as when Samuel de Champlain first explored them in the early 1600s. A large portion of the state is still forest land. Hundreds of its lakes and ponds have no houses on their shores. Indeed, enough of Maine exists as it once was that we can, even today, envision what this place must have been when all of it was untamed.

Have you ever listened to loons calling at night on Nahmakanta Lake? Watched the rising sun light the face of Mount Kineo on the shores of Moosehead? Cruised the "Bold Coast" as thrashing green blue waters foam over ancient granite headlands?

Have you ever kicked your feet into the sandy

—AMONG THE MANY AREAS PROTECTED BY THE MAINE COAST HERITAGE TRUST ARE SEVERAL ISLANDS IN MUSCONGUS BAY.

—DURING THE MOOSE RUT, BULLS OFTEN SPAR WITH EACH OTHER.—

beach of Burnt Island in Penobscot Bay under the watchful eye of bald eagles on a sunny July morning? Strolled past fields flooded with the rare Northern Blazing Star flower at Kennebunk Plains on a late August afternoon? Or watched a bull moose feeding at a remote pond in Baxter State Park as a crystal clear October day dawns?

If you've been lucky enough to enjoy any of these experiences, you may have wondered how the wild and natural splendor of such special places has survived in in a world where progress is often defined by the number of houses that we can jam onto an acre of land.

Is the Maine that we love in danger of vanishing? Can the state's wildness possibly survive in a world increasingly controlled by global corporations, outside political influences, sprawling development, and mushrooming demands on natural resources? Every time we build a house or a school or a mall, we dis-place nature. Of course we all need a place to live and to work and to shop for necessities. But the character of truly special places must be preserved.

*Saving Maine* tells the story of how some of the

—THE WATERBORO BARRENS PRESERVE, PROTECTED BY THE NATURE CONSERVANCY

12    —Nahmakanta Lake and its surrounding forest, protected by
the Land for Maine's Future Program—

—Sunkhaze Meadows National Wildlife Refuge, protected with the assistance of
The Nature Conservancy—

state's most wild lands and waters have been protected for future generations. While the book could have included any number of such places, those selected are here because I found them unique while pursuing my career, nature photography.

Nearly every land-protection project is a long, involved process and involves innumerable details. I deliberately omitted such minutiae to keep the focus on the contributions of the people who spearheaded these efforts and on the beauty of the places they sought to preserve. In so doing, I hope to have created a book not just for conservationists but for all who love Maine.

Bill Silliker Jr.
Saco, Maine

LOOKING DOWN ON THE RHYOLITE CLIFFS OF MOUNT KINEO, THE JEWEL OF MOOSEHEAD LAKE—

—Joseph Deering and his family donated half of the Saco Heath
to The Nature Conservancy.—

15

—GETTING TO GREEN FALLS, IN THE HEART OF BAXTER STATE PARK, REQUIRES A DAY'S HIKE.—

# Nature at Peace

STARTING IN 1919, Maine Governor Percival P. Baxter sought to convince the state legislature that the wild lands around Katahdin—"Greatest Mountain" in the Penobscot Indian language—were so special that they should be purchased for a state park "to be held as a great primitive recreational area and wildlife sanctuary."

Baxter was eloquent in defense of his idea. In just one of many speeches he delivered on the subject, he said in 1921, "Maine is famous for its twenty-five hundred miles of seacoast, with its countless islands; for its myriad lakes and ponds; and for its forests and rivers. But Mount Katahdin Park will be the state's crowning glory, a worthy memorial to commemorate the end of the first and the beginning of the second century of Maine's statehood.

"This park will prove a blessing to those who follow us, and they will see that we built for them more wisely than our forefathers did for us."

On this last point, Baxter was passionate. He was outraged at the way that Maine's wild lands, which once belonged to the people of the state, had been sold irresponsibly and "for trifling sums per acre" in deals perpetrated by land speculators, unscrupulous timber companies, and shortsighted government officials. Baxter pointed out that almost three million acres were given away to the railroads in 1868.

He asked one audience of Maine sportsmen, "Is it not fitting that, upon payment of a fair price, the grandest and most beautiful portion of all this great area which the people of the state once possessed, should again become their property?"

The answer from the legislature was a resounding no.

So Percival Baxter set out to buy that special place himself, acre by acre, parcel by parcel.

Percival Baxter put only his own money into the creation of this most unusual park during the course of a sixty-year process that continued even after his death, thanks to a fund that he left for further land

acquisitions. He began in 1930 with a $25,000 purchase of six thousand acres that included Katahdin. He then gave that tract to the state, to be held in trust as "forever wild" by the people of Maine. In 1931 the legislature named the park he had begun to amass in the heart of the Maine woods in his honor.

The story of his efforts tells much about what one man with foresight can accomplish if he has the will, the perseverance, and the means. Baxter was heir to a fortune, a wealthy man for sure, but a man careful with that money. He dickered well to get the lands that he put into his park. The effort consumed most of his energies and much of his family fortune.

It wasn't easy. Some opposed him at every opportunity. Others ridiculed him as a fool to buy the burned-over and logged-out wastelands that most of these acres were considered to be.

Political enemies challenged his efforts, both in the Maine statehouse and at the federal level, and their number included some who proposed that Baxter's gift be turned into a national park. But that couldn't be done because he had carefully crafted deeds of trust that controlled his gifts of land to the state over the years.

Baxter was no fan of federal involvement in state

NESOWADNEHUNK STREAM
ON A SUMMER EVENING—

—The Ledges, one of many waterfalls in Baxter State Park—

—Katahdin, donated to the people of Maine by Percival Baxter—

—Katahdin seen from Sandy Stream Pond—

affairs. While he supported the concept of Maine's national park at Acadia—still called Lafayette National Park while Percival Baxter was governor—he apparently didn't trust the process, having witnessed too many times how governments can change the rules of the game unless bound by documents such as those he created to protect his park.

It may well have been a concern that the federal government might pursue a park in the Maine woods that drove Baxter to continue land acquisition long after Katahdin itself was protected. In so doing, he created a much larger park, one that likely dwarfs anything that the National Park Service might have done. Today Baxter State Park comprises over two hundred thousand acres, an astounding gift from a single man to the people of Maine.

Most in his time appreciated Baxter's efforts and thanked him for his generosity. Many in our time point to his vision as an inspiration that they and others have followed. In 1999, Maine Governor Angus King referred to Percival Baxter's gift as, "probably the most extraordinary example of an individual's generosity in the history of this country."

It is worth noting that the lands surrounding the

A HIKER'S VIEW OF KATAHDIN, LOOKING INTO THE GREAT BASIN FROM BLUEBERRY KNOLL—

two rivers Percival Baxter referred to in his speeches—the Penobscot and the St. John—are at the heart of two major land-protection efforts today. Those timberlands have been cut over again and again, including the creation of some large clearcuts, and the construction of gravel logging roads that crisscross parts of them. Nonetheless, much of that acreage remains as undeveloped as it was during Percival Baxter's time.

A few final words from his 1921 speech make one pause to marvel at his foresight. (Keep in mind that it took nearly a week to reach Katahdin from Bangor in those days, requiring a combination of train, boat, canoe, horseback, and foot travel.)

"This park will prove a great attraction, not only to the people of Maine who will frequent it, but also to those who come from without our state to enjoy the free life of the out of doors. The park will bring health and recreation to those who journey there, and the wildlife of the woods will find refuge from their pursuers, for the park will be made a bird and game sanctuary for the protection of its forest inhabitants."

Over the years road access to this part of Maine has greatly improved, and many people have come to treasure this special wilderness. As Park Director Irvin

"Buzz" Caverly stated in 1999, "It is important that we as Maine people, and generations that follow, take care of this precious gift because it is the most unique ever received by a citizenry."

Percival Baxter had the foresight to realize that part of our natural heritage should be left intact for future generations. But he was wrong about one thing: "Someday—maybe in your day—there won't be any really wild areas left. This park may be the only place where future generations can see Maine as it really was."

Fortunately other segments of "Maine as it really was" still remain, thanks in large part to the efforts of people who have followed Baxter's example. As we shall see, his generosity, patience, and perseverance have motivated others to work to keep what is special about Maine from vanishing. ▨

SPRUCE GROUSE, TAMER BUT LESS OFTEN SEEN COUSIN OF THE RUFFED GROUSE—

—A MOTHER MOOSE BONDS WITH HER NEWBORN CALVES.

—A view from the summit of Cadillac Mountain—

# The Gold Coast

**BOSTON-AREA RESIDENT** Charles Eliot had an intense love of nature. Probably because of that, he forged a worldwide reputation as a landscape architect while still a young man. A disciple of Frederick Law Olmsted, the "father" of New York City's Central Park, Eliot gained experience that made him concerned about the loss of large areas of open space in the Boston metropolitan area during the late 1800s.

These concerns led to the founding of a group that had a new idea for land preservation—buying still-pristine tracts with private funds and holding them in trust for the public. That group incorporated in the state of Massachusetts in 1891 as the Trustees of Public Reservations. Still in existence (now as the Trustees of Reservations), this private land trust—the first in the nation—has protected more than thirty thousand acres in Massachusetts.

Eliot next set his sights on protecting what he thought was the most remarkable part of Maine. Both the beauty of the state's rocky coast and its vulnerability to development had long impressed him. His love of Maine had evolved during his childhood summers, when Charles and his brother sailed extensively with their father in the Mount Desert Island area. Later, while a student at Harvard, he formed the Champlain Society, a group dedicated to the scientific research and historical study of that region.

Eliot's was an age of unchecked wealth and power. It was also an era when many of the newly rich people "from away" were building their exclusive summer playgrounds along the Maine coast. Eliot's concern about their impact on the beauty of the natural landscape was matched by his worry that native Mainers were being priced out of the real-estate market, displaced by land speculators. He feared that the day would come when the average person would not have access to the "seaside wilderness of Maine."

Charles Eliot never got to follow through with his hopes to protect Maine's coast. He contracted meningitis and died at thirty-eight years of age. But his dream stayed alive through the efforts of his father, Charles W. Eliot, the president of Harvard University from 1869 to 1909. The senior Eliot was one of the well-to-do summer residents of the Acadia region, having built his home at Asticou on the advice of his son Charles.

In 1901, three years after his namesake's death, Charles W. Eliot hosted a meeting on an August evening during which he encouraged the village-improvement societies of Seal Harbor, Bar Harbor, and Northeast Harbor to work together to protect the natural beauty of Mount Desert Island. He proposed that they do that by establishing the Hancock County Board of Trustees of Public Reservations.

A key participant in that meeting was George Dorr, a wealthy Boston bachelor who had the time, the resources, the connections, and—most important—the persistence to work on a grand project proposed by a proud father in memory of a dearly beloved son.

Today we know that undertaking as Acadia National Park.

The complete story of the park is a long and intricate one, as are the stories of most such conservation efforts. It began when Dorr picked up Eliot's challenge. It continued as he spent the rest of his life and his entire fortune in the effort to fulfill what so suddenly became his dream that summer night.

As described in its charter, obtained from the Maine Legislature in 1903, the purpose of the Hancock County Board of Trustees of Public Reservations was "to acquire, by devise, gift or purchase, and to own, arrange, hold, maintain, or improve for public use lands in Hancock County, Maine, which by reason of scenic beauty, historical interest, sanitary advantage, or other like reasons may become available for such purpose." While Dorr worked almost single-handedly at the realization of that goal, wealthy neighbors and friends helped the process by giving parcels of land to the newly created organization.

The most famous of those individuals, John D. Rockefeller Jr., not only donated more than eleven thousand acres, he also paid for the design and construction of Acadia's nearly sixty miles of carriage roads, which are still in use today. Rockefeller much preferred horses to the recently invented automobile

—THE MOON SETS BEHIND THE PRECIPICE.—

as the way to move around in the park and the surrounding area. He wanted to provide access to its
spectacular views in a way that intruded least on its
fragile landscape.

Many summer residents favored outlawing the
use of automobiles in the region and were able to
establish bans in several of the more affluent communities. But controversy over the restrictions on cars
pitted these people "from away" against some of the
year-round residents, and there were repercussions. In
1913, a bill before the Maine legislature sought to
nullify the charter of the Hancock County Trustees of
Public Reservations, perhaps to discourage any interest in renewing the bans on automobiles, perhaps in
retribution for them.

Whatever the motive, that move failed. But the
realization that local and state interests might undo his
grand project prompted Dorr to convince Eliot that
they must protect the lands of the Trustees by turning
ownership over to the United States government.

After considerable lobbying by Dorr, that
exchange occurred on June 10, 1916. First protected
as Sieur de Monts National Monument under the
"Act for the Preservation of American Antiquities,"

ACADIA COAST
ON A WINTER MORNING—

—Champlain Mountain seen from Schooner Head Road—

29

—Winter paints Acadia National Park's rugged coast.—

—A LONE HIKER PROVIDES SCALE TO THE IMMENSITY OF THIS PROTECTED COASTLINE.—

the holdings became the first national park east of the Mississippi River in 1919. When President Woodrow Wilson signed the act establishing Lafayette National Park, he called Dorr's efforts "the greatest of one-man shows in the history of land conservation."

The park was expanded and renamed Acadia in 1929. A British landowner had agreed to adding her holdings at Schoodic Head to the park on condition that it would not continue to bear the name of the French general who had helped the colonies to gain independence from her home country.

IT'S IRONIC that the continuing proliferation of automobiles and their exhaust gases again threaten this natural place. In response, the National Park Service recently implemented a voluntary program involving propane-powered tour buses and may yet ban private vehicles on Acadia's paved roads, as it has in several other national parks.

But if that happens, access to Acadia's beauty won't be lost. Many miles of hiking trails traverse the park, and Mr. Rockefeller's carriage roads—long enjoyed by hikers, bicyclers, and those with horses— look better with each passing year. ▣

ALONG THE SHORE DRIVE OF
ACADIA NATIONAL PARK—

# Old Growth

IN THE MID 1980s, Alan Hutchinson, at the time a biologist with the Maine Department of Inland Fisheries and Wildlife, got an intriguing telephone call one evening: Would he be available the next morning to fly over a stretch of the Maine woods north of Baxter State Park? Alan agreed to meet the caller, John Jensen of the Maine Chapter of The Nature Conservancy, at the airport in Old Town.

Jensen had arranged for a small plane to take them over an unusual parcel of Maine woods owned by the Pingree family and managed for them by the Seven Islands Land Company. Beginning in the 1840s, the Pingrees built a tradition of conservative forest management that led to their being widely recognized in Maine as a leader in sustainable tree harvesting. Jensen had been contacted by a longtime forester for the family, John Sinclair, who inquired about The Nature Conservancy's possible interest in protecting the parcel.

He told Jensen that any plan to protect this land would be complicated, if it could even be done at all. Complex legal concerns and serious tax consequences might be involved. Any discussions about the possibility would also have to be kept strictly confidential.

Why was such secrecy required?

A bit of Maine woods history explains. For many decades, timber harvesting in the state was focused relatively close to rivers or streams, even ones where water flow was seasonal, so that the logs could be floated downriver to market. The Pingree land in question lay far from any adequate water sources, so generations of Maine loggers had passed it by in favor of areas where the timber was easier to move.

When John Sinclair first looked at the Pingrees' isolated stand of mature trees, he saw a forest that had not yet been cut. The approximately five thousand acres of mixed hardwoods and softwoods of the Big Reed Pond region truly represented an old-growth forest, which by some definitions requires that a stand be at least 150 years old.

—THE NATURE CONSERVANCY'S
BIG REED FOREST RESERVE

—ON THE TRAIL IN THE BIG REED FOREST—

But the parcel's isolation was coming to an end. After of log drives on Maine's waterways were banned in the 1970s, due to concerns about pollution and erosion, landowners began building gravel roads to provide access to additional stands of harvestable timber. By the 1980s, the Big Reed parcel was only about five miles from the nearest road. Sinclair knew that it was only a matter of time before a road would pass close enough to this unique patch of forest that it would become attractive for harvesting.

He then convinced the Pingree heirs that they must find a way to protect these woods. But concerns that public awareness of such a large expanse of old-growth forest in Maine might invite interference from radical environmentalists that would be detrimental to their efforts led to the quiet approach to The Nature Conservancy.

As many are aware, this organization protects land the old-fashioned way: It purchases tracts of land to protect the diversity of wildlife or unusually valuable habitat there. The Nature Conservancy prides itself on its nonconfrontational, nonpartisan, solution-oriented approach to conservation challenges. A private, international, nonprofit organization established in 1951 to

— TREES LIVE OUT THEIR
NATURAL EXISTENCE IN THESE
NEVER-HARVESTED WOODS.

—THE BIG REED FOREST RESERVE PROTECTS SOME FIVE THOUSAND ACRES OF TRUE OLD GROWTH, THANKS TO THE FORESIGHT OF A PINGREE FAMILY FORESTER.—

—An old-growth forest from above—

preserve plants, animals, and unique natural communities, The Nature Conservancy today owns and manages the largest private system of nature sanctuaries in the world.

When contacted by forester Sinclair, John Jensen was chair of the Maine Chapter's land-protection committee. He asked Alan Hutchinson to go along on the overflight that day partly because of the biologist's experience in protecting habitat for Maine's Endangered and Threatened Species Program and partly because Hutchinson was also a trustee of The Nature Conservancy. Jensen hoped that their combined expertise might enable them to draft a plan to protect the old-growth forest around Big Reed Pond.

And draft it they did—on a placemat in a restaurant in Old Town. As they waited for a delayed breakfast that morning, Jensen and Hutchinson sketched out an idea on the handiest bit of paper they could find. Their concept included a swap with the Maine Bureau of Public Lands.

Brad Wellman, president of the Seven Islands Land Company, later presented a fleshed-out transfer-of-ownership plan to The Nature Conservancy and the Bureau of Public Lands. It involved a trade of

TREES LINE THE SHORES OF
BIG REED POND. —

harvestable timberlands, plus some funds, for the Big Reed forest.

The Nature Conservancy then launched a major fundraising drive to help pay for the transaction, a campaign that was helped by a $50,000 grant from the L. L. Bean company.

The Big Reed Forest Reserve is such a vulnerable, wild place that no marked trails approach it. The Nature Conservancy prefers that any visits be first authorized by one of its staff to minimize possible adverse impacts on this remote forest. The organization does periodically offer guided field trips.

But you don't have to go to the Big Reed Reserve in person to appreciate that in the heart of Maine there is still a forest that has never been cut. Ever. ▪

—BLACK BEARS INHABIT THESE WOODS
BUT ARE SELDOM SEEN.

# The Bold Coast

"YOU GET OUT ON the mossy ground on
that knoll there . . . I've always thought that if there
was someplace on Earth where God wanted to come
down and view his handiwork, he'd be right there."
As his boat rolled in the swells, that's how lobsterman
Jasper Cates described a beautiful piece of Maine's
"Bold Coast," which runs for thirty-five miles from
Cutler to Lubec.

His description helps to explain why Cates
fought so hard to save 247 acres on the Western Head
and Great Head peninsulas from what seemed an
unwise development project. Aside from changes to
the landscape, Cates feared the pollution that would
result if a subdivision of expensive homes was built on
that poorly drained, rockbound land.

His ties to this part of the down east coast are
strong ones. The first Cates settled on the sheltered
harbor of Cutler in 1785, one of the original four
families to do so. A Cates has trapped, trawled, or
seined for the region's marine resources ever since.
And so the family has an intense regard for this

MUCH OF MAINE'S BOLD COAST
REMAINS AS WILD TODAY AS WHEN
SAMUEL DE CHAMPLAIN EXPLORED
IT IN THE EARLY 1600S. —

—A LOBSTER BOAT WORKS THE WATERS OFF CUTLER.—

rugged stretch of shoreline. Jasper Cates's affection for this wild place has led him on journeys he never imagined he'd take when he pulled his first lobster trap from its cold waters. One of them was showing this stretch of granite headlands to Peggy Rockefeller.

Rockefeller, whose father-in-law, John D. Rockefeller Jr., helped to establish Acadia National Park on Mount Desert Island, saw the same beauty that Jasper Cates so eloquently describes. And, like Cates, she recognized how vulnerable it was to development.

It was in the late 1960s that Peggy Rockefeller first became concerned about the increase in home construction that she witnessed along the Maine coast. She foresaw that the down east region, and especially its islands, might soon experience intense development pressure.

She also understood the tradition of private ownership, one that many Mainers hold dear. She knew that even if the state ever found the money to acquire some of this shoreland, many owners would not be interested in selling what they considered to be part of their heritage. While that ethic had worked for centuries to keep the Maine coast relatively un-developed, Rockefeller could see that, before long,

RUGGED HEADLANDS MEET THE OCEAN
ALONG MAINE'S FARTHEST
DOWN EAST COAST. —

—The efforts of a variety of conservation organizations helped to protect the Bold Coast.—

tradition would not be enough to save it. The thinking of newer generations was different. Development
pressures were growing. Something had to be done.

Rockefeller knew that conservation easements had
been used successfully by the Trustees of Reservations
in Massachusetts. Easements place legal restrictions
on a parcel's development rights while allowing the
owners to retain it as private property. While some
landowners might agree to a "forever wild" status for
an entire parcel, others might opt for limiting development rights on ecologically sensitive portions while
permitting moderate development or some other
activity, such as sustainable forestry, on other parts.
Conservation easements might be donated, generally
with tax advantages for the landowner, or they might
be sold.

Rockefeller was quick to see how effective
conservation easements would be in preserving
traditional ownership and cultural heritage on the
coast of Maine, while at the same time protecting
the land.

She found a staunch ally in Tom Cabot, a wealthy
industrialist and philanthropist from one of Boston's
oldest families. He was an adventurer who loved the
outdoors—and especially sailing down east. He had

HARBOR SEALS ENJOY A ROCKY LEDGE
ON A SUNNY DAY. —

—The Maine Coast Heritage Trust has protected more than 325 islands and 110,000 acres.—

long recognized that someday the islands along Maine's coast could become overdeveloped, so he began buying those which he found most vulnerable, even as far back as the 1930s and 40s.

In 1970, Peggy Rockefeller teamed up with Tom Cabot and a few others to form an organization that would focus on using donated conservation easements to maintain private ownership of coastal land while protecting its public values forever. They named their group the Maine Coast Heritage Trust.

Not surprisingly, the organization's initial efforts focused on the Acadia region. Rockefeller herself granted an easement on Buckle Island to Acadia National Park. She and her husband later gave the park an easement of more than a thousand acres around Long Pond in Seal Harbor.

It was to the Maine Coast Heritage Trust that Jasper Cates turned when he sought help to save the headlands in the Cutler region. But the Bold Coast needed more than conservation easements to protect it. The would-be developer of the parcel that had inspired Cates to get involved wasn't about to give up on the project. His land had a market value in the millions of dollars. Other, equally vulnerable stretches of

the down east coast had caught the eye of developers as well.

The late 1980s were bringing change to Maine, as a surging demand for vacation homes in fragile coastal areas threatened to destroy the essence of what attracts people to the state in the first place.

The effort to protect the Bold Coast also brought change to the Maine Coast Heritage Trust. Recognizing that development pressures had increased to the point that some places could not be protected by conservation easements alone, the group decided to set up a revolving fund so that it would always have ready cash to buy land that was in imminent danger. When the idea of such a fund was first discussed, Peggy Rockefeller said: "Yes, we should try to raise two million dollars. How about five million?"

In April 1988, MCHT board members Ben Emory, Bruce Jacobsen, and others began a fund-raising campaign to do just that.

Jasper Cates says he'll never forget the day he took Peggy Rockefeller along the Cutler shoreline in his lobster boat. He showed her the land slated for the big housing project and told her how much the developer wanted to be paid not to build there. Peggy

— TERNS NESTING ON SOME DOWN EAST ISLANDS BENEFIT FROM THE FISHERIES FOUND IN THE HEALTHY WATERS ALONG THE BOLD COAST.

Rockefeller patted Jasper on the back and said, "Don't you worry. We'll find a way."

Part of the solution involved her donating a million dollars of her own money to the revolving fund. While that impressed Cates, what first endeared Peggy Rockefeller to him was that she had gone to the trouble to do the breakfast dishes for Jasper's wife, Cutler's postmistress, who had left for work while Cates himself was out readying his boat for Rockefeller's morning tour.

In December 1988 the Maine Coast Heritage Trust purchased the Great Head and Western Head peninsulas. MCHT also worked with several other land conservation groups and the state's fledgling Land for Maine's Future Program to develop a purchase plan that ultimately protected more than ten thousand acres and many important stretches of shoreline along the the Bold Coast. That plan included setting aside two hundred acres suitable for the development of affordable housing in the town of Cutler.

While the protection of the Bold Coast utimately required the outright purchase of land, Peggy Rockefeller and the Maine Coast Heritage Trust

didn't give up on using the all-important conservation easement. On the contrary, Rockefeller so believed in the concept that she urged MCHT to help organize and support local land trusts. In that way, she reasoned, others could do similar good work in their own backyards. The result was MCHT's Land Trust Program, which originated in 1987.

Today, eighty-six land trusts are working to protect the wildness of Maine, up from fewer than twenty such groups in the 1970s. As MCHT president Jay Espy describes this effort: "Saving land at the local level is one of the most tangible things that people can do. A land trust can protect more land for less money through creative solutions that benefit landowners and the public than with most other methods known to man. A land trust empowers people to actively save those places in their community that they value the most."

Jasper Cates would tell you that you don't have to be a millionaire or business executive to participate. Or, as Espy says, "Land-conservation people come in all flavors. When it comes to protecting open space, it tends to be a unifying activity. We all benefit from it."

A COMMON TERN LANDS AT ITS NEST. —

48    —THE MOUTH OF GOOSEFARE BROOK OPENS INTO THE ATLANTIC BETWEEN OCEAN PARK AND SACO.—

# A Friend in Need

"EVERYONE KNOWS that there's nothing out there but seagulls."

Those few words spoken at a 1986 Saco planning board meeting fired up a group of citizens who wanted to keep some of southern Maine the way it was. In the real estate boom of the mid-1980s, developers focused on the open stretches of Maine's southern coast as ideal places to build vacation homes. One subdivision proposal after another swamped small-town planning boards and threatened natural resource areas. None of the communities caught in the sudden storm had ordinances in place that were adequate to protect their coastlines.

Especially vulnerable were the upland edge of transitional habitat and the smaller of the freshwater wetland areas adjacent to southern Maine's handful of saltwater estuaries. Both the estuaries and the wetlands provide vital food, cover, and breeding habitat for migratory waterfowl, wading birds, and songbirds. Many of these crucial acres were already on a "wish list" for inclusion in the Rachel Carson National Wildlife Refuge. But the U.S. Fish and Wildlife Service had no funds with which to purchase them, and no laws protected them from development.

One of the largest of the development proposals called for a thousand dwelling units—vacation condos, year-round homes, a convention center, and more. This single project would have affected some five hundred acres of the critical upland that buffers the Saco side of the Goosefare Marsh. While the developers had the best of intentions, they overlooked the fact that such a huge project, no matter how carefully done, would alter or destroy important wildlife habitat.

It is easy to understand why some Saco residents questioned the wisdom of making such a major change in the nature—literally—of the Goosefare Marsh and its upland, which had survived pretty much intact since the days when the Sokokis, or Saco Indians, hunted and fished there. A significant part of

— The Goosefare Brook Division of the Rachel Carson National Wildlife Refuge,
one of five national wildlife refuges in Maine. —

—HUNDREDS OF BUILDINGS WERE ONCE PLANNED TO BE BUILT IN THESE WOODS
ON THE EDGE OF THE GOOSEFARE MARSH.—

what was special about Saco would surely vanish forever.

As with most such controversial issues, both sides based their arguments on protection of people's rights. The landowners had development rights. Respect for private property rights has been a long-standing principle of our laws. But how much development do such rights allow? And how do those rights balance against the rights of the community to protect natural areas that have an influence on the quality of life for all residents?

Increasing development pressures raised questions that local governments in southern Maine had not faced before. What are a community's rights when it comes to controlling the cumulative impact of development? A house here or there seems to make only a minor impact, but as more landowners exercised their right to build on their acres, the collective result was beginning to devastate natural areas. In the mid-1980s, few communities had yet enacted zoning and planning laws, perhaps because many Mainers share both a penchant for independent thinking and a dislike for government interference in their affairs.

One neighborhood group—Alan and Nan Cone,

SIGNIFICANT WILDLIFE HABITAT FLANKS
THE MEANDERING GOOSEFARE BROOK
AS IT FLOWS TO THE SEA.—

Horace and Phyllis Wood, Sue and Mark Sladen, and others—decided to organize as the Saco Citizens Coalition in order to research how the proposed thousand-unit development project could affect the natural resources of the Goosefare Marsh. Like most Saco citizens, they had assumed that since a small sign proclaimed the marsh to be part of the Rachel Carson National Wildlife Refuge, it must be already protected from development. Horace Wood soon found out that only the half-acre parcel on which the sign was posted was actually protected

Because of southern Maine's coastal geography, the Rachel Carson National Wildlife Refuge is strung out in ten divisions scattered from Kittery to Cape Elizabeth. Most of them protected only marshland at that time.

Members of the coalition began appearing at local public meetings to make carefully worded statements about the resource values of the Goosefare. They also contacted community, state, and federal officials, and the press. They brought along photographs of the Goosefare Marsh to clearly and vividly show what was at risk. And they asked: "What about the Rachel Carson Refuge?"

—DESPITE ITS LOCATION ADJACENT TO A GOLF COURSE AND OTHER DEVELOPMENT, MOST OF THIS NATURAL AREA HAS SURVIVED WITH MINIMAL IMPACT FOR HUNDREDS OF YEARS.

The efforts of the Saco Citizens Coalition attracted others, including the owners of one of Saco's last dairy farms, Jim and Edna Leary. Voices from all across the community were raised as a more and more people began to question the wisdom of such a grand development scheme.

Always the focus was on the positive, however. The SCC's bumper stickers read, "Save the Marsh," not "Ban Condos" or some similarly negative proclamation. They weren't out to totally stop the development, but to control it adequately to protect the resource and to keep some of what was special about Saco from disappearing forever.

As with all such land protection efforts, the story is not as simple as a brief description makes it sound. The developers' ambitious plan was supported by some in the community, including many in local government who thought it offered progress and an economic boon. There was also the legal question of whether zoning land for resource protection constitutes an unconsitiutional "taking" of private land without just compensation.

The SCC hired Attorney Jeffrey Thaler to research this issue and provided him with a pile of

documents: local ordinances, pages on the history of the marsh, and comments by experts on the specific natural resources at risk in the Goosefare Marsh. One of the many stamps the postal clerk stuck on the thick envelope showed the likeness of Rachel Carson. It seemed like an omen: somehow the Saco Citizens Coalition was going to win.

Then, as months dragged into years and SCC members appeared at meeting after meeting, always with new challenges to face, it often seemed that their efforts were futile. Finally, in 1989, their perseverance paid off: the coalition's consistent efforts attracted the attention of the Maine Chapter of The Nature Conservancy. This larger, more experienced organization—which incidentally was cofounded by Rachel Carson in the 1950s—borrowed 2.3 million dollars and quietly purchased all five hundred acres intended for that Goosefare Marsh development project. At that time, it was their largest purchase in the state of Maine.

This purchase was a holding action, the plan being that the land would ultimately become part of the Rachel Carson National Wildlife Refuge. This presented The Nature Conservancy with a good deal

— MINK AND BLUE-WINGED TEAL ARE AMONG THE MANY WILDLIFE TRANSIENTS THAT USE THE GOOSEFARE MARSH ECOSYSTEM.

of risk, as they could only hope that the U.S. Fish and Wildlife Service someday would have the funds to pay them back. The Saco Citizens Coalition members next turned their energies to getting commitments from Maine's entire Congressional delegation to see that the Fish and Wildlife Service got the necessary funding as soon as possible.

With the assistance of several key individuals, including Cherie Mason from the Maine Sierra Club and Andrew French, then manager of the Rachel Carson National Wildlife Refuge, the Saco Citizens Coalition had by then also spawned another organization: the Friends of Rachel Carson National Wildlife Refuge. Formed in 1987, this group brought together concerned residents from all the Maine communities that were home to the ten divisions of this far-flung refuge. The Friends' primary mission has been to see that the RCNWR continues to get the federal money and support it needs to complete its land acquisition plans. The fairest and best way to protect these special acres, the Friends of the Rachel Carson National Wildlife Refuge believe, is to buy land from willing sellers and encourage gifts from owners who can afford to donate their land.

The funds for these purchases are not tax dollars; they come from the Land and Water Conservation Fund, revenues for which come from federal oil and gas leases. Congress established the fund to protect key natural resource lands.

The Saco Citizens Coalition has long since disbanded, its work done. But the Friends of Rachel Carson National Wildlife Refuge continues, and it has been a friend indeed. When the group first organized, the Rachel Carson National Wildlife Refuge had received only $650,000 for land acquisition from the Land and Water Conservation Fund. Thanks in part to the efforts of the Friends, as of this writing the RCNWR has been granted more than $20 million in land acquisition funding and has grown from some three thousand acres to more than five thousand. ■

BLUE-WINGED TEAL—

—Mount Kineo towers over Moosehead Lake.—

# Political Will and Public Good

"SOME DAY, fifty or a hundred years from now, a family will come ashore at Mount Kineo, camp, spend the night, see the sun rise over that remarkable feature, and they won't know us, they won't remember our names, but they will experience something that is—to say "uplifting" is an understatement—it's the essence of our humanity and our relationship to the land and to nature."

Maine governor Angus King's 1998 response to a question about why he felt the Land for Maine's Future Program was so important echoed comments he'd made when running for his first term in 1994.

In neither instance was King simply paying lip service to the Land for Maine's Future Program. While still a private citizen, and as host of a public affairs program on Maine Public Television, King was the official spokesman and a highly visible supporter of a 1987 referendum campaign in favor of a $35 million bond issue to create and fund an agency to purchase lands of statewide significance for recreation

and conservation. That broadly successful referendum established the Land for Maine's Future Program.

King had earlier served on Governor Joseph Brennan's Commission on Outdoor Recreation, in 1986. As a result of their research, the commissioners recommended state acquisition of lands of natural significance, and ultimately the development of the Land for Maine's Future Program. King was a lead author of their report.

At that time, Maine had one of the lowest rates of public conservation land ownership in the nation. Part of the reason for that situation was a chronic lack of funding for acquisition of significant conservation lands. According to it's legislative mandate, the program's purpose is to acquire lands of state significance, lands that "make a substantial and lasting contribution toward assuring all of Maine's citizens, present and future, the traditional Maine heritage of public access to Maine's land and water resources [and toward maintaining] quality and availability

of natural resources important to the interests . . . of Maine people."

The program did just that. By 1997, the spectacular places that Land for Maine's Future had protected included coastal islands; a stretch of the Bold Coast; portions of the Kennebunk Plains, a grassland habitat where a rare flower blooms and an even rarer song sparrow nests; working farmland; pristine Nahmakanta Lake and more than thirty thousand forested acres around it; and, of course, Mount Kineo. In all, the LMF program had, in ten short years, protected 63,355 acres in 45 separate projects.

With the initial money nearly gone, Governor King and a league of conservation organizations launched another referendum campaign in 1999, this time to raise $50 million more. The solid support of Maine's citizens was evidenced by the fact that the referendum passed by a nearly 70% yes vote and was approved in every one of the state's sixteen counties.

Additional revenues come in from from a special credit card, issued by MBNA, that pays a royalty to the LMF Program. In his first gubernatorial campaign, King had proposed such an affinity card, one he referred to as the "Katahdin card," believing that

BURNT ISLAND PROVIDES HABITAT FOR A VARIETY OF COASTAL SEABIRDS. —

—In the spirit of Percival Baxter's gift to the people of Maine, the Land for Maine's Future Program protects special places that offer a variety of recreational opportunities for future generations.—

—The Lubec sandbar provides significant habitat for migrating shore birds.—

—Rising above Cobscook Bay, Shackford Head offers spectacular ocean views.—

—THE RARE NORTHERN BLAZING STAR BLOOMS IN LATE AUGUST ON THE KENNEBUNK PLAINS.—

Maine's "Greatest Mountain" would be a good image to show on a card that helped raise money for land protection.

King made good on that campaign pledge in 1996 by establishing the nation's first state-sponsored credit card for public land acquisition. This program enables cardholders to give a little bit to conservation as they make their purchases.

Through the Land For Maine's Future Program, we collectively can follow the example set by Percival Baxter, explains Governor King, who has said that his participation in its creation will always be one of his proudest achievements. Private land protection often closes off areas from public access, but Land for Maine's Future assures that today's citizens can share with future generations "the Maine that has meant so much to all of us." ■

—THE SHORE OF NAHMAKANTA LAKE

—GREEN MOUNTAIN OVERLOOKS THE NORTH BRANCH OF THE PENOBSCOT RIVER.—

# Whose Woods Are These?

**"I SEE LOTS OF TREES,"** says Hank Swan when asked about his vision for the Maine woods. "Lots of trees and gentler harvesting methods."

When Hank Swan talks about his view for the future of the north woods, those who love Maine should listen. Swan is the chairman of Wagner Forest Management, a company presently managing nearly two million acres of commercial forest lands in Maine. These lands include much of the country Henry David Thoreau wrote about in *The Maine Woods*. Such names as North East Carry, Lobster Stream, Chesuncook Lake, and West Branch of the Penobscot River show on Wagner's land maps.

Institutional investors and foundations only recently started becoming owners of large stretches of Maine forest lands. That represents a significant change. For more than a century, timber barons, paper mills, and industrial landowners owned some ten million acres of the north Maine woods.

Most of these lands had originally belonged to the citizens of Maine. In the words of Percival Baxter, "The greater part of these lands was once the property of the people of this State, and, had our forefathers handed down to us this great domain, what a transformation would have been wrought in the life and institutions of our State!" Perhaps that's part of the reason why a tradition of public access to privately owned lands has existed since the days when Henry David Thoreau made his trips to the Maine woods.

Of course, the timber-harvesting landowners had another incentive for allowing people to use their lands for hunting and fishing and other recreational activities: they needed the cooperation of the people who lived nearby and who worked in the forest and the mills. "The public feel that they have an ownership stake," is how Hank Swan puts it. "The paper companies, with their partly paternalistic approach, tolerated the public who wanted to use these woods to hike, hunt, fish, and camp."

—CLEARCUTS, A CONTROVERSIAL HARVESTING METHOD, HAVE BEEN BETTER CONTROLLED IN MAINE
SINCE THE TIME WHEN THIS PHOTOGRAPH WAS MADE, IN THE EARLY 1990S.—

—LOWER-IMPACT METHODS OF HARVESTING MAKE FOR A BETTER USE OF THE FOREST RESOURCE.—

But today, it is less common for the paper mills to grow their own wood on their own lands. How long will the tradition of public access continue when the interests of new landowners lie more in realizing a relatively quick return on their investment than in providing a long-term, consistent timber supply for the mills? And what might happen should paper mill owners, most now having divested themselves of these lands, decide to pull up stakes to seek greener forests and more profitable markets?

Those concerns, and the prospect that "the political scene might someday invite radical solutions," helped drive Hank Swan to act on his vision for the future of these woods. He's been guiding the owners of the lands his company manages toward conservation easement agreements that could protect close to a million acres of Maine's big woods from development, while reserving the owners' timber management rights.

What type of forest management should it be? In Swan's view, "We need to work the woods harder and smarter. But we don't have to disregard stewardship to do that. Sustainability. You never cut more than the land is capable of growing—the ability of the forest to do its job. You want to protect water quality, wildlife, and the habitat."

Improved mechanization can result in less stand damage and improved worker safety, Swan believes. He's convinced that both of these goals can be achieved while contributing to the local forest community economies, especially if more secondary wood products and processing are pursued. "We're not aggressively finding ways to use the forest. We need more value-added secondary manufacturing."

As for traditional recreation values, Swan notes a change in the culture of many who come to play in these woods. "They want easy access to do whatever their thing is. The old generations that came to the backwoods sporting camps are rapidly disappearing." When one thinks of modern society's proliferation of acronym toys—SUVs, ORVs, ATVs, PWCs, not to mention snowmobiles and big motorboats—it's hard to disagree. All this motorized access adds to the challenge of keeping Maine's big woods relatively "wild."

While Swan thinks that wood harvesting can be done by more mechanized methods, he says it must also be done with greater concern for the visual results. "My forestry brethren chose to ignore the visual side of forestry for years. We were unsmart as a profession, and some even had an 'in your face' attitude towards the public. We need to use gentler harvesting methods—cut more to length at the stump—be absolutely less intrusive on the landscape. Appearance matters."

At times Swan sounds almost like a hard-core environmentalist, but in fact he takes a pragmatic approach that recognizes the long tradition of privately owned "working" forest land in this part of the Northeast. That's why he believes that conservation easements are often the best way to balance the many interests involved in the future of these lands.

That view disappoints those who prefer a more pristine, wilderness status for all of those distant wooded acres or who seek to create a Maine woods national park. But Swan thinks it's better for landowners to work now with the "environmental centrists" rather than possibly face a difficult future situation should radical environmental groups gain sufficient political clout to instigate the "taking" of conservation lands without adequate compensation to landowners. He believes that conservation easements protect both the integrity of the forests and the local economies that

—Big Spencer Mountain is included
in the lands protected by the
Forest Society of Maine.

have depended on those forests for more than a century. With easements in place, "the forests are going to remain intact. We're not going to see development and fragmentation." To Hank Swan, that provides significant conservation benefits.

Others apparently agree with him. A conservation easement sold by the Pingree Forest Partnership to the New England Forestry Foundation in March 2001 protected 762,192 acres of northern Maine forests. Thanks to that one agreement, the shorelines of 110 pristine lakes, some 2,000 miles of river frontage, and 1,191 square miles of forest will never be developed.

The West Branch Easement project of the Forest Society of Maine is another example. The society hopes to ultimately protect 685,000 acres in the region between Moosehead Lake and Baxter State Park, including many places that Thoreau trekked through on the way to Chesuncook.

The purchase of key land parcels by the various conservation organizations active in Maine has also been a part of the recent efforts to protect the integrity of the historic "Maine Woods." The Nature Conservancy has purchased an entire ecosystem:

THE BRANCHING PENOBSCOT RIVER
REACHES DEEP INTO MAINE'S
NORTH WOODS. —

185,000-plus acres surrounding the wild St. John River. Several landmarks, including Big Spencer Mountain and more than twelve miles of shoreline along Moosehead Lake, have been protected by purchase in the first phase of the Forest Society of Maine's efforts. The Trust for Public Land has negotiated purchase agreements on behalf of the state of Maine for several areas in the northern forest, including a large part of the eastern shoreline of Moosehead Lake.

Hank Swan says that he himself "has come full circle." A graduate of the University of Maine at Orono, where he studied forestry, Swan worked as an assistant ranger for the U.S. Forest Service in the White Mountain National Forest before launching a financial management career that ultimately led him to Wagner Forest Management. He takes pride in calling himself a conservationist.

Those who think that the only way to protect the classic Maine woods is by turning them into a national park will never agree with Swan's vision, but one thing none can deny: Hank Swan cares deeply about the future of both the forest and the people who find work and recreation there. ▧

—THE BABBLING OF A BROOK IN AN OTHERWISE QUIET STRETCH OF WOODS IS A TREASURE TO ENJOY.

—THE CONFLUENCE OF THE SHEEPSCOT RIVER AND ITS WEST BRANCH—

# The Logger, the Dam Breaker, and the Widget Maker

**WHEN MAINE FORESTER** and logger John Wentzel was asked to evaluate a parcel of land in Whitefield, he didn't realize he'd become a player in a conservation story that grows in significance with each passing year. The out-of-state landowner had contacted Wentzel to survey the damage on her land caused by the massive ice storm of 1998. She wanted his advice on the likelihood of salvage harvesting the timber still standing there, and what that might bring for revenue.

When Wentzel turned off Route 17 onto narrow Howe Road to visit the property, he was surprised at how wild and wooded the lands along that country road appeared. He wondered why he'd not been through that area before.

The feeling that he was visiting a special place really hit him when he walked the parcel. The land he had been asked to evaluate bordered both the West Branch of the Sheepscot River and the Sheepscot River itself. Its shorelines formed the northern boundary of the confluence of the two rivers.

And as he walked, John Wentzel imagined a different time. Having studied the history of Maine's original peoples, he was aware that ancient canoe routes once brought fishing and hunting parties down these rivers. With relatively short overland portages, Native Americans could travel from the Kennebec River to China Lake and then to the West Branch of the Sheepscot.

Historically, the Sheepscot waters that border the property have provided spawning habitat and oxygen-rich pools for trout, Atlantic salmon, and other fish. The upland edge has provided riparian habitat for a variety of wildlife. And the parcel, although it had been cut selectively over the years, was still a wild place that benefited those same resources today.

As a trained forester, Wetzel believes in the sustainable harvesting of timber for the many wood products that society requires. But here he faced a curious moment. He could earn a paycheck for drawing up the complicated forestry management plan required to properly harvest wood from this riverside

—WOODED UPLAND ALONG THE WEST BRANCH OF THE SHEEPSCOT RIVER

73

property, but he thought enough about this unique location that he decided to research the issue a bit further before any cutting was done. He asked the landowner exactly what she wanted to achieve by having the timber harvested. When she told him that she just wanted to get some money from her land and would consider selling the parcel instead, he told her that he might know someone she should talk to.

Wentzel was thinking of his neighbor, Chris Hamilton, Communications Director for the Maine Coast Heritage Trust. He told Hamilton of the parcel's importance as wildlife habitat, and how he figured that it would be better preserved than harvested.

Hamilton referred the matter to the Sheepscot Valley Conservation Association, which had already protected several adjacent stretches of the Sheepscot through a conservation easement from the landowner, Coastal Enterprises, Inc. By granting the conservation easement, Coastal Enterprises gave up the right to harvest wood from the land and assured that future owners also will not engage in woodcutting there. Remarkably, the company did not ask for a corresponding reduction of their property taxes. Steven Cole of Coastal Enterprises said that the company wanted to help protect these watershed acres to

THE SHEEPSCOT PROVIDES
SIGNIFICANT HABITAT FOR
VARIOUS FISHES. —

benefit the Sheepscot's fish spawning habitat by minimizing siltation and maintaining the cooling influence of the upland forest cover along the river banks.

Thanks to such efforts, the Sheepscot Valley Conservation Association, a regional land trust, now protects nearly a mile of river habitat that is vital to the maintenance of a healthy trout fishery and the hoped-for recovery of the endangered Atlantic salmon.

What is inspiring about the story of John Wenztel is that he is not "an environmentalist," in the sense that many people would use that label. But, as with many of the other folks who have worked to keep special places in Maine unspoiled, when Wentzel recognized the opportunity to do something to protect a significant wild place, he did it.

**RECOGNIZING AND ACTING** on such opportunities lie at the root of all conservation efforts. And sometimes significant conservation milestones aren't the actions that keep a hitherto unspoiled place pristine. Sometimes we can repair past damage and help bring back a bit of wildness.

Perhaps the best example of that was the removal of the Edwards Dam in 1999. The Edwards Dam, on the Kennebec River in Augusta, had blocked the upstream migration of anadromous fish such as salmon, shad, and sturgeon for 160 years. When it was built in 1837, the dam included a fish ladder designed to permit migration of spawning fish, but that soon washed out and was never rebuilt. The dam continued to block the flow of the Kennebec for years, even after becoming become a dinosaur of sorts when its meager power-generation capability was no longer needed and the textile mill it once powered was long-since defunct.

Edwards Dam was overdue for its periodic re-licensing, and when its owners sought a forty-year renewal from the Federal Regulatory commission, Everett "Brownie" Carson, Executive Director of the Natural Resources Council of Maine, was among those who saw the opportunity to bring back a special part of Maine's environment. Carson led NRCM to join with other environmental and sporting groups to form the Kennebec Coalition. Together they worked to get the dam removed.

A CROWD OF DIGNITARIES PARTICIPATED IN THE CEREMONY AT THE REMOVAL OF EDWARDS DAM, WHICH WAS THE CULMINATION OF THE EFFORTS OF SEVERAL ORGANIZATIONS. —

—The Edwards Dam blocked the Kennebec River for a century and a half.—

—After the initial breach, and the eventual removal of the old dam, the Kennebec once more flowed freely from Augusta to the sea.—

Thanks to the coalition's concerted efforts, the Federal Energy Regulatory Commission ordered the dam's demolition in 1997. Its owners challenged the order at first, but finally agreed to transfer ownership to the state of Maine as a gift so the dam could be removed. Funding for the project came from the Kennebec Hydro Developers Group (owners of other dams further upriver) and Bath Iron Works (as part of a mitigation agreement for BIW development downriver).

The removal of Edwards Dam in 1999 marked the first time ever that an operating dam for which the owners had sought relicensing was ordered to be retired and removed, as it was no longer the best option for the resource represented by the Kennebec River.

**DOING SOMETHING** to protect the best examples of Maine's remaining unspoiled lands sometimes is just a matter of giving of one's time. I can think of no better example than the several pilots who have volunteered their time to fly me all across the state as I documented Maine's wild lands on film for The Nature Conservancy, the Maine Coast

—RIVER OTTER

Heritage Trust, the Trust for Public Land, the Forest Society of Maine, and regional and local land trusts. I have had the pleasure of meeting Spike Haible, Rudy Engholm, and Steve Williams—small plane owners who donate their time, the use of their planes, and sometimes even the gas, in an effort to help keep Maine the special place that it is today.

Steve Williams may have put it best when asked why he takes time away from managing his own business, Woodex Bearing Company, which makes a variety of wooden parts for machinery, to do his part to help save some of what's special about Maine. He replied that he wasn't great at making speeches, wasn't a polished writer, and didn't much care to go to meetings, but he knew he could help by flying photographers over the undeveloped stretches of Maine to get the images that show a lot of other folks what is there to be saved.

SO THERE WE HAVE IT: a logger, a dam breaker, and a widget maker—three individuals representing different approaches to conservation in Maine. ▪

—SEVERAL PILOTS HAVE HELPED THE AUTHOR TO OBTAIN AERIAL PHOTOGRAPHS OF MAINE'S SPECIAL PLACES.

—The St. John, the most unspoiled river east of the Mississippi.—

# A Legacy that Lasts

KENT WOMMACK had six weeks to do what had taken Percival Baxter sixty years to accomplish. As executive director of the Maine Chapter of The Nature Conservancy, Wommack had a chance to forever protect 185,000 acres of the Maine woods from development, if he could find 35 million dollars in a month and a half.

Never before had a land protection effort of such size been attempted in such a short time. But the possibility that The Nature Conservancy might protect a forty-mile stretch of the St. John—the wildest river east of the Mississippi—and the undeveloped forest that surrounds it, drove Wommack to explore where none had gone before. Even the Maine Chapter's internationally recognized parent organization had never taken on a project so costly, not to mention one with such a short timetable.

Like Percival Baxter, Wommack had a personal vision that helped him to see light through the trees of a seemingly impenetrable forest. Unlike Baxter, he had a lot of help. First, he had the inspiration of former Governor Baxter himself. Wommack believes that Baxter's example helped individual donors make the decision to give huge sums to the St. John River effort. As he puts it: "How many of us will ever have the opportunity to leave the lasting legacy that Percival Baxter did? We all want to do something meaningful—to leave a mark. But how many of us will ever have that chance?"

That chance arose when The Nature Conservancy put together an agreement with a timberland investment firm for a small share in the purchase of a large woodland parcel that International Paper was selling. Had that transaction gone through as planned, The Nature Conservancy's participation would have protected the river frontage, but two corporate bidders sent in higher offers.

Then, in late November 1998, Wommack got a telephone call. Due to a complicated set of circumstances, the offers of both of the higher bidders had

fallen through; would the conservancy still be interested making the purchase—the whole deal—all by itself? If so, it had to find 35.1 million dollars by the year's end.

Their former timberland investment partner had by then committed its monies elsewhere. Wommack sought help from The Nature Conservancy's national office, promising the national board that if they made a $35.1 million loan from their Land Preservation Fund—a revolving land protection contingency account—the Maine Chapter would raise ten million dollars in pledges in six weeks or the deal was off.

Wommack showed them maps of the huge undeveloped woods and the wild river. John Sawhill, then president of The Nature Conservancy, immediately understood the opportunity to protect an entire ecosystem and responded: "How could we not do it?" The conservancy's board agreed.

Wommack and the Maine Chapter then had the seemingly impossible task of securing those pledges. How did they do it? Wommack thinks it helped that this project offered an unmatched opportunity for those who love Maine to collectively do something that they couldn't have done individually. "This is not

After the spring freshet has subsided, the St. John looks quiet, but the rocks make formidable rapids when the river is at full flood. —

about me. This is about people coming together around a vision that we together can fulfill. The real heroes here are the people who stepped forward with huge contributions."

Among the leaders in raising funds in this huge effort were Lisa and Leon Gorman. (Gorman is the grandson of Maine entrepreneur L.L. Bean.) Several others pledged a million dollars each.

The Maine Chapter found several additional million-dollar donors when Kent Wommack sought help from the Maine Coast Heritage Trust. In a classic example of inspired leadership, MCHT's president, Jay Espy, solicited support from his own organization's major donors. Three members of the Rockefeller family, including David Rockefeller, Sr., widower of Peggy Rockefeller, and Dr. Richard Rockefeller, her son, contributed to the project to protect the ecosystem of the St. John River.

Helping someone else's project says a lot about an organization. It also says something about the way people feel about Maine. The concept of the greater good overrides any thought about protecting someone's individual turf.

These early commitments gave the huge project

—FLOWERS BLOOM ALONG
THE RIVER BOTTOM.

84　　　—The St. John, filled with snowmelt and spring rainwater just after ice out—

—Both shores of the St. John will remain "forever wild" for some sixty miles, thanks to the leadership of The Nature Conservancy.—

—CANADA LYNX HAVE BEEN
FOUND DENNING IN THE
ST. JOHN REGION.

a solid start. Maintaining that momentum and raising another 25 million dollars would seem to be a daunting task, yet the Maine Chapter raised the rest of the money to pay off their loan within two years.

Proving once again that one doesn't have to be wealthy to participate in the effort to save what's best about Maine, these additional funds came from many different sources. Gifts from families, foundations, and corporations benefited the project, as did the continuing support of thousands of Nature Conservancy members, sending in a few dollars at a time.

The Maine Chapter then went on to secure additional agreements with three other landowners that, once completed, will protect by ownership or conservation easement some 450,000 acres of the St. John region. These agreements include protecting another seventeen miles of the St. John with a thousand-foot corridor of trees on both sides of the river that will never be cut again.

With this effort, The Nature Conservancy has fulfilled a significant conservation vision. This vision—that well-chosen reserves representing the full range of diverse native habitats should be set aside, while neighboring lands support well-managed

sustainable forestry activities—provides a model for other large-scale land protection efforts. The conservancy has protected an entire ecosystem here, not just a parcel, and it has demonstrated that such a mix of forest uses can work to protect the most fragile parts of the St. John River tract while permitting appropriate forestry uses on the less vulnerable areas. In the process, the organization has also committed to securing permanent public access for traditional recreational activities in that region.

Kent Wommack says that he and The Nature Conservancy also made an important discovery in the process: "We discovered that we have an obligation to give people who love Maine the opportunity to protect its most special places." Collectively we can do things as grand as the accomplishment of Percival Baxter, Wommack believes. As the director of The Nature Conservancy in Maine, he sees it as his duty to help us to do it. ▪

# Conclusion

**IN A 1921 SPEECH** to the Maine Sportsmen's Fish and Game Association, Percival Baxter, then president of the state senate, described his dream for a wilderness park in the heart of the Maine woods. In his speech, Baxter told of a unique feature: "To most people, Mount Katahdin is but a name. To those who have both seen and climbed the mountain, it is a wonderful reality, and the memories of a trip to its summit remain vivid through the years."

Perhaps even more vivid than a trip to the summit of Katahdin is the example that Baxter himself set when, lacking any official backing from the legislature, he singlehandedly made that wilderness park a reality. As we have seen, his example has convinced others that they too can make a difference in protecting the special place we call Maine. And Percival Baxter's accomplishments are not ended; other conservation success stories may well lie ahead as his example continues to inspire protection of more and more Maine sites.

88 — OLD-GROWTH WHITE PINES IN THE HERMITAGE PRESERVE, ONE OF MORE THAN EIGHTY PRESERVES
IN MAINE OWNED BY THE NATURE CONSERVANCY. —

Baxter didn't give up on his dream. Neither did Charles Eliot and George Dorr; nor did Peggy Rockefeller. But does one have to be a wealthy Baxter, Dorr, or Rockefeller to make a difference in preserving Maine's natural character?

On the contrary. Most of the work of saving the best of Maine comes from the efforts of just plain folks. You could be one of them. ▪

—COMMON LOON FAMILY

—THE FOREST MEETS THE SEA AT THE BOLD COAST OF MAINE

—Sunkhaze Stream—

# *Appendix*

LISTED BELOW are a few key organizations that are helping to save Maine's special places, but many other local land trusts, environmental organizations, and nature groups are working at a variety of efforts too numerous to describe here. For a more complete list of such organizations, contact the State Planning Office or look on the Internet.

Appalachian Mountain Club
5 Joy Street
Boston, MA 02108

Forest Society of Maine
P.O. Box 775, 115 Franklin Street
Bangor, ME 04402

Friends of Acadia
P.O. Box 45
Bar Harbor, ME 04609

Friends of Baxter State Park
P.O. Box 152
Millinocket, ME 04462

Friends of Rachel Carson National Wildlife Refuge
P.O. Box 427
Ocean Park, ME 04063

Land for Maine's Future Program
State Planning Office
38 State House Station
184 State St.
Augusta ME 04333

Maine Audubon Society
20 Gilsland Farm Road
Falmouth, Maine 04105

Maine Chapter of The Nature Conservancy
Fort Andross
14 Maine Street, Suite 401
Brunswick, ME 04011

Maine Coast Heritage Trust
Bowdoin Mill
One Main Street
Topsham, ME 04086

92    —MORE OF MAINE'S NATURAL AREAS REMAIN TO BE PROTECTED. WE, IN OUR TIME, HAVE LEARNED THAT WE CAN PROVIDE FOR FUTURE GENERATIONS MORE WISELY THAN OUR FOREFATHERS DID FOR US.—

Maine Land Trust Network, c/o MCHT,
Bowdoin Mill,
One Main Street,
Topsham, ME 04086

Natural Resources Council of Maine
3 Wade Street
Augusta, ME 04330

New England Forestry Foundation
P.O. Box 1099,
283 Old Dunstable Road
Groton, MA  01450-3099

The Sierra Club Maine Chapter
One Pleasant Street
Portland, ME 04101-3936

The Trust For Public Land
Maine Field Office
245 Commercial Street
Portland, ME 04101

The Wilderness Society
45 Bromfield St., Suite 1101
Boston, MA 02108

# *Acknowledgments*

IN VARIOUS WAYS, many other people helped to make this book a reality.

Dave Morine and Bruce Kidman, of The Nature Conservancy, read the first draft of this text and suggested ways to make *Saving Maine* a better book. Chris Hamilton, of Maine Coast Heritage Trust, offered encouragement and generously gave his own time to help research several of the stories.

Some of the scenic photographs for this book were made with a GSW 690 panoramic camera made available by my friends at Fujifilm Professional, and I could not have captured the aerial images without the expertise of the pilots who have flown me safely over Maine's special places.

My heartfelt thanks go to these people and to all the others, too numerous to mention here, who are helping to save the best of Maine for today and tomorrow.

—Bill Silliker, Jr.

**AS A SPECIAL OFFERING,** the following images from *Saving Maine* are available as archival quality prints on 16 x 20-inch paper for $125 each (Maine residents include 5% sales tax), digitally signed by Bill Silliker, Jr. A portion of the proceeds from the sale of each print will be donated to the organization listed below the image.

Order a print on line at:
www.savingmaine.com

Order by mail from:
Bill Silliker, Jr.
Wildlife & Nature Photography
P.O. Box 7106
Ocean Park, ME  04063

THE FRIENDS OF BAXTER STATE PARK
*(jacket image)*

THE FRIENDS OF ACADIA
*(back jacket image)*

THE NATURE CONSERVANCY
*(image on page 36)*

THE LAND FOR MAINE'S FUTURE PROGRAM
*(image on page 56)*

THE FRIENDS OF THE RACHEL CARSON
NATIONAL WILDLIFE REFUGE
*(image on page 48)*

THE MAINE COAST HERITAGE TRUST
*(image on page 40)*

—Tracy Pond, Baxter State Park, with Katahdin in the distance—